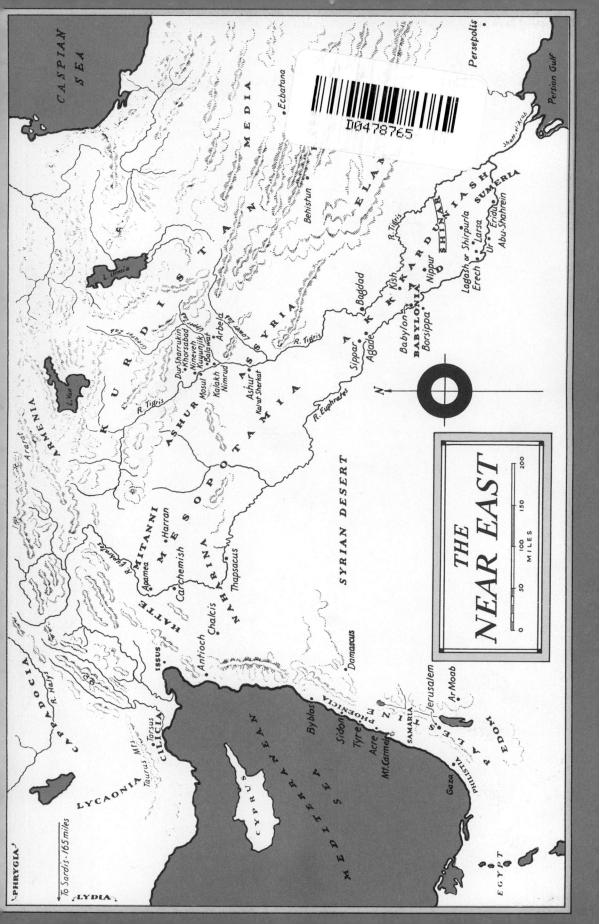

THE
NEAR EAST

MILES
0   50   100   150   200

The Story of Civilization

PART ONE

OUR ORIENTAL HERITAGE

OUR ORIENTAL HERITAGE

Being a history of civilization in Egypt and the Near East
to the death of Alexander, and in India, China and Japan
from the beginning to our own day; with an introduction
on the nature and foundations of civilization

By Will Durant

SIMON AND SCHUSTER

NEW YORK : 1954

Library of Congress Catalog Card Number 35–10016

PRINTED IN THE UNITED STATES OF AMERICA BY
KINGSPORT PRESS, INC., KINGSPORT, TENNESSEE

TO ARIEL

Preface

I HAVE tried in this book to accomplish the first part of a pleasant assignment which I rashly laid upon myself some twenty years ago: to write a history of civilization. I wish to tell as much as I can, in as little space as I can, of the contributions that genius and labor have made to the cultural heritage of mankind—to chronicle and contemplate, in their causes, character and effects, the advances of invention, the varieties of economic organization, the experiments in government, the aspirations of religion, the mutations of morals and manners, the masterpieces of literature, the development of science, the wisdom of philosophy, and the achievements of art. I do not need to be told how absurd this enterprise is, nor how immodest is its very conception; for many years of effort have brought it to but a fifth of its completion, and have made it clear that no one mind, and no single lifetime, can adequately compass this task. Nevertheless I have dreamed that despite the many errors inevitable in this undertaking, it may be of some use to those upon whom the passion for philosophy has laid the compulsion to try to see things whole, to pursue perspective, unity and understanding through history in time, as well as to seek them through science in space.

I have long felt that our usual method of writing history in separate longitudinal sections—economic history, political history, religious history, the history of philosophy, the history of literature, the history of science, the history of music, the history of art—does injustice to the unity of human life; that history should be written collaterally as well as lineally, synthetically as well as analytically; and that the ideal historiography would seek to portray in each period the total complex of a nation's culture, institutions, adventures and ways. But the accumulation of knowledge has divided history, like science, into a thousand isolated specialties; and prudent scholars have refrained from attempting any view of the whole—whether of the material universe, or of the living past of our race. For the probability of error increases with the scope of the undertaking, and any man who sells his soul to synthesis will be a tragic target for a myriad merry darts of specialist critique. "Consider," said Ptah-hotep five thousand years ago, "how thou mayest be opposed by an expert in council. It is

vii

foolish to speak on every kind of work."* A history of civilization shares the presumptuousness of every philosophical enterprise: it offers the ridiculous spectacle of a fragment expounding the whole. Like philosophy, such a venture has no rational excuse, and is at best but a brave stupidity; but let us hope that, like philosophy, it will always lure some rash spirits into its fatal depths.

The plan of the series is to narrate the history of civilization in five independent parts:

I. *Our Oriental Heritage:* a history of civilization in Egypt and the Near East to the death of Alexander, and in India, China and Japan to the present day; with an introduction on the nature and elements of civilization.

II. *Our Classical Heritage:* a history of civilization in Greece and Rome, and of civilization in the Near East under Greek and Roman domination.

III. *Our Medieval Heritage:* Catholic and feudal Europe, Byzantine civilization, Mohammedan and Judaic culture in Asia, Africa and Spain, and the Italian Renaissance.

IV. *Our European Heritage:* the cultural history of the European states from the Protestant Reformation to the French Revolution.

V. *Our Modern Heritage:* the history of European invention and statesmanship, science and philosophy, religion and morals, literature and art from the accession of Napoleon to our own times.

Our story begins with the Orient, not merely because Asia was the scene of the oldest civilizations known to us, but because those civilizations formed the background and basis of that Greek and Roman culture which Sir Henry Maine mistakenly supposed to be the whole source of the modern mind. We shall be surprised to learn how much of our most indispensable inventions, our economic and political organization, our science and our literature, our philosophy and our religion, goes back to Egypt and the Orient.† At this historic moment—when the ascendancy of Europe is so rapidly coming to an end, when Asia is swelling with resurrected life, and the theme of the twentieth century seems destined to be an all-embrac-

* Cf. p. 193 below.

† The contributions of the Orient to our cultural heritage are summed up in the concluding pages of this volume.

ing conflict between the East and the West—the provincialism of our tra-ditional histories, which began with Greece and summed up Asia in a line, has become no merely academic error, but a possibly fatal failure of per-spective and intelligence. The future faces into the Pacific, and under-standing must follow it there.

But how shall an Occidental mind ever understand the Orient? Eight years of study and travel have only made this, too, more evident—that not even a lifetime of devoted scholarship would suffice to initiate a Western student into the subtle character and secret lore of the East. Every chap-ter, every paragraph in this book will offend or amuse some patriotic or esoteric soul: the orthodox Jew will need all his ancient patience to forgive the pages on Yahveh; the metaphysical Hindu will mourn this superficial scratching of Indian philosophy; and the Chinese or Japanese sage will smile indulgently at these brief and inadequate selections from the wealth of Far Eastern literature and thought. Some of the errors in the chapter on Judea have been corrected by Professor Harry Wolfson of Harvard; Dr. Ananda Coomaraswamy of the Boston Institute of Fine Arts has given the section on India a most painstaking revision, but must not be held responsi-ble for the conclusions I have reached or the errors that remain; Professor H. H. Gowen, the learned Orientalist of the University of Washington, and Upton Close, whose knowledge of the Orient seems inexhaustible, have checked the more flagrant mistakes in the chapters on China and Japan; and Mr. George Sokolsky has given to the pages on contemporary affairs in the Far East the benefit of his first-hand information. Should the public be indulgent enough to call for a second edition of this book, the opportunity will be taken to incorporate whatever further corrections may be suggested by critics, specialists and readers. Meanwhile a weary author may sympathize with Tai T'ung, who in the thirteenth century issued his *History of Chinese Writing* with these words: "Were I to await perfec-tion, my book would never be finished."*

Since these ear-minded times are not propitious for the popularity of ex-pensive books on remote subjects of interest only to citizens of the world, it may be that the continuation of this series will be delayed by the prosaic necessities of economic life. But if the reception of this adventure in syn-thesis makes possible an uninterrupted devotion to the undertaking, Part Two should be ready by the fall of 1940, and its successors should appear,

---

* Carter, T. F., *The Invention of Printing in China, and Its Spread Westward;* New York, 1925, p. xviii.

by the grace of health, at five-year intervals thereafter. Nothing would make me happier than to be freed, for this work, from every other literary enterprise. I shall proceed as rapidly as time and circumstance will permit, hoping that a few of my contemporaries will care to grow old with me while learning, and that these volumes may help some of our children to understand and enjoy the infinite riches of their inheritance.

WILL DURANT.

Great Neck, N. Y., March, 1935

A NOTE ON THE USE OF THIS BOOK

To bring the volume into smaller compass certain technical passages, which may prove difficult for the general reader, have been printed (like this paragraph) in reduced type. Despite much compression the book is still too long, and the font of reduced type has not sufficed to indicate all the dull passages. I trust that the reader will not attempt more than a chapter at a time.

Indented passages in reduced type are quotations. The raised numbers refer to the Notes at the end of the volume; to facilitate reference to these Notes the number of the chapter is given at the head of each page. An occasional hiatus in the numbering of the Notes was caused by abbreviating the printed text. The books referred to in the Notes are more fully described in the Bibliography, whose starred titles may serve as a guide to further reading. The Glossary defines all foreign words used in the text. The Index pronounces foreign names, and gives biographical dates.

It should be added that this book has no relation to, and makes no use of, a biographical *Story of Civilization* prepared for newspaper publication in 1927-28.

ACKNOWLEDGMENTS

I am grateful to the following authors and publishers for permission to quote from their books:

Leonard, W. E., *Gilgamesh;* the Viking Press.
Giles, H. A., *A History of Chinese Literature;* D. Appleton-Century Co.
Underwood, Edna Worthley, *Tu Fu;* the Mosher Press.
Waley, Arthur, *170 Chinese Poems;* Alfred A. Knopf.
Breasted, Jas. H., *The Development of Religion and Thought in Ancient Egypt;* Scribner's.
Obata, Shigeyoshi, *Works of Li Po;* E. P. Dutton.
Tietjens, Eunice, *Poetry of the Orient;* Alfred A. Knopf.
Van Doren, Mark, *Anthology of World Poetry;* the Literary Guild.
"Upton Close," unpublished translations of Chinese poems.

x

Contents

INTRODUCTION

THE ESTABLISHMENT
OF CIVILIZATION

Chapter I: THE CONDITIONS OF CIVILIZATION....................................... 1

Definition — Geological conditions — Geographical — Economic — Racial — Psychological — Causes of the decay of civilizations

Chapter II: THE ECONOMIC ELEMENTS OF CIVILIZATION.................. 5

I. FROM HUNTING TO TILLAGE, 5
Primitive improvidence—Beginnings of provision—Hunting and fishing—Herding—The domestication of animals—Agriculture—Food—Cooking—Cannibalism

II. THE FOUNDATIONS OF INDUSTRY, 11
Fire—Primitive Tools—Weaving and pottery—Building and transport—Trade and finance

III. ECONOMIC ORGANIZATION, 16
Primitive communism—Causes of its disappearance—Origins of private property—Slavery—Classes

Chapter III: THE POLITICAL ELEMENTS OF CIVILIZATION................ 21

I. THE ORIGINS OF GOVERNMENT, 21
The unsocial instinct—Primitive anarchism—The clan and the tribe—The king—War

II. THE STATE, 23
As the organization of force—The village community—The psychological aides of the state

III. LAW, 25
Law-lessness—Law and custom—Revenge—Fines—Courts—Ordeal—The duel—Punishment—Primitive freedom

IV. THE FAMILY, 29
Its function in civilization—The clan vs. the family—Growth of parental care—Unimportance of the father—Separation of the sexes—Mother-right—Status of woman —Her occupations—Her economic achievements—The patriarchate—The subjection of woman

xi

Chapter IV: THE MORAL ELEMENTS OF CIVILIZATION...................... 36

    I. MARRIAGE, 36
    The meaning of marriage—Its biological origins—Sexual communism—Trial marriage
    —Group marriage—Individual marriage—Polygamy—Its eugenic value—Exogamy—
    Marriage by service—By capture—By purchase—Primitive love—The economic func-
    tion of marriage

    II. SEXUAL MORALITY, 44
    Premarital relations — Prostitution — Chastity — Virginity — The double standard —
    Modesty — The relativity of morals — The biological rôle of modesty — Adultery —
    Divorce—Abortion—Infanticide—Childhood—The individual

    III. SOCIAL MORALITY, 51
    The nature of virtue and vice—Greed—Dishonesty—Violence—Homicide—Suicide—
    The socialization of the individual—Altruism—Hospitality—Manners—Tribal limits of
    morality—Primitive vs. modern morals—Religion and morals

    IV. RELIGION, 56
    Primitive atheists

        1. THE SOURCES OF RELIGION
        Fear—Wonder—Dreams—The soul—Animism

        2. THE OBJECTS OF RELIGION
        The sun — The stars — The earth — Sex — Animals — Totemism — The transition to
        human gods—Ghost-worship—Ancestor-worship

        3. THE METHODS OF RELIGION
        Magic — Vegetation rites — Festivals of license — Myths of the resurrected god —
        Magic and superstition—Magic and science—Priests

        4. THE MORAL FUNCTION OF RELIGION
        Religion and government—Tabu—Sexual tabus—The lag of religion—Secularization

Chapter V: THE MENTAL ELEMENTS OF CIVILIZATION.................... 72

    I. LETTERS, 72
    Language—Its animal background—Its human origins—Its development—Its results—
    Education—Initiation—Writing—Poetry

    II. SCIENCE, 78
    Origins—Mathematics—Astronomy—Medicine—Surgery

    III. ART, 82
    The meaning of beauty—Of art—The primitive sense of beauty—The painting of the
    body — Cosmetics — Tattooing — Scarification — Clothing — Ornaments — Pottery —
    Painting — Sculpture — Architecture — The dance — Music — Summary of the
    primitive preparation for civilization

Chronological Chart: Types and Cultures of Prehistoric Man........ 90

Chapter VI: THE PREHISTORIC BEGINNINGS OF CIVILIZATION.......... 90

    I. PALEOLITHIC CULTURE, 90
        The purpose of prehistory—The romances of archeology

        1. MEN OF THE OLD STONE AGE
            The geological background—Paleolithic types

        2. ARTS OF THE OLD STONE AGE
            Tools—Fire—Painting—Sculpture

    II. NEOLITHIC CULTURE, 98
        The Kitchen-Middens—The Lake-Dwellers—The coming of agriculture—The taming
        of animals—Technology—Neolithic weaving—pottery—building—transport—religion—
        science—Summary of the prehistoric preparation for civilization

    III. THE TRANSITION TO HISTORY, 102

        1. THE COMING OF METALS
            Copper—Bronze—Iron

        2. WRITING
            Its possible ceramic origins — The "Mediterranean Signary" — Hieroglyphics —
            Alphabets

        3. LOST CIVILIZATIONS
            Polynesia—"Atlantis"

        4. CRADLES OF CIVILIZATION
            Central Asia—Anau—Lines of Dispersion

BOOK ONE

THE NEAR EAST

Chronological Table of Near Eastern History............................... 113

Chapter VII: SUMERIA... 116
    Orientation—Contributions of the Near East to Western civilization

    I. ELAM, 117
        The culture of Susa—The potter's wheel—The wagon-wheel

    II. THE SUMERIANS, 118

        1. THE HISTORICAL BACKGROUND
            The exhuming of Sumeria—Geography—Race—Appearance—The Sumerian Flood
            —The kings—An ancient reformer—Sargon of Akkad—The Golden Age of Ur

        2. ECONOMIC LIFE
            The soil—Industry—Trade—Classes—Science

        3. GOVERNMENT
            The kings—Ways of war—The feudal barons—Law

        4. RELIGION AND MORALITY
            The Sumerian Pantheon—The food of the gods—Mythology—Education—A Sume-
            rian prayer—Temple prostitutes—The rights of woman—Sumerian cosmetics

5. LETTERS AND ARTS
Writing — Literature — Temples and palaces — Statuary — Ceramics — Jewelry—
Summary of Sumerian civilization

III. PASSAGE TO EGYPT, 134
Sumerian influence in Mesopotamia — Ancient Arabia — Mesopotamian influence in
Egypt

Chapter VIII: EGYPT.. 137

I. THE GIFT OF THE NILE, 137
1. IN THE DELTA
Alexandria—The Nile—The Pyramids—The Sphinx

2. UPSTREAM
Memphis—The masterpiece of Queen Hatshepsut—The "Colossi of Memnon"—
Luxor and Karnak—The grandeur of Egyptian civilization

II. THE MASTER BUILDERS, 144
1. THE DISCOVERY OF EGYPT
Champollion and the Rosetta Stone

2. PREHISTORIC EGYPT
Paleolithic—Neolithic—The Badarians—Predynastic—Race

3. THE OLD KINGDOM
The "nomes"—The first historic individual—"Cheops"—"Chephren"—The purpose
of the Pyramids—Art of the tombs—Mummification

4. THE MIDDLE KINGDOM
The Feudal Age--The Twelfth Dynasty—The Hyksos Domination

5. THE EMPIRE
The great queen—Thutmose III—The zenith of Egypt

III. THE CIVILIZATION OF EGYPT, 156
1. AGRICULTURE

2. INDUSTRY
Miners — Manufactures — Workers — Engineers — Transport — Postal service —
Commerce and finance — Scribes

3. GOVERNMENT
The bureaucrats—Law—The vizier—The pharaoh

4. MORALS
Royal incest—The harem—Marriage—The position of woman—The matriarchate in
Egypt—Sexual morality

5. MANNERS
Character—Games—Appearance—Cosmetics—Costume—Jewelry

6. LETTERS
Education—Schools of government—Paper and ink—Stages in the development of
writing—Forms of Egyptian writing

7. LITERATURE
Texts and libraries—The Egyptian Sinbad—The Story of Sinuhe—Fiction—An
amorous fragment—Love poems—History—A literary revolution

CONTENTS

8. SCIENCE
Origins of Egyptian science—Mathematics—Astronomy and the calendar—Anatomy and physiology—Medicine, surgery and hygiene

9. ART
Architecture—Old Kingdom, Middle Kingdom, Empire and Saïte sculpture—Bas-relief—Painting—Minor arts—Music—The artists

10. PHILOSOPHY
The *Instructions of Ptah-hotep*—The *Admonitions of Ipuwer*—The *Dialogue of a Misanthrope*—The Egyptian Ecclesiastes

11. RELIGION
Sky gods—The sun god—Plant gods—Animal gods—Sex gods—Human gods—Osiris—Isis and Horus—Minor deities—The priests—Immortality—The *Book of the Dead*—The "Negative Confession"—Magic—Corruption

IV. THE HERETIC KING, 205
The character of Ikhnaton—The new religion—A hymn to the sun—Monotheism—The new dogma—The new art—Reaction—Nofretete—Break-up of the Empire—Death of Ikhnaton

V. DECLINE AND FALL, 213
Tutenkhamon—The labors of Rameses II—The wealth of the clergy—The poverty of the people—The conquest of Egypt—Summary of Egyptian contributions to civilization

Chapter IX: BABYLONIA 218

I. FROM HAMMURABI TO NEBUCHADREZZAR, 218
Babylonian contributions to modern civilization—The Land between the Rivers—Hammurabi—His capital—The Kassite Domination—The Amarna letters—The Assyrian Conquest—Nebuchadrezzar—Babylon in the days of its glory

II. THE TOILERS, 226
Hunting — Tillage — Food — Industry — Transport — The perils of commerce — Money-lenders—Slaves

III. THE LAW, 230
The Code of Hammurabi—The powers of the king—Trial by ordeal—*Lex Talionis*—Forms of punishment—Codes of wages and prices—State restoration of stolen goods

IV. THE GODS OF BABYLON, 232
Religion and the state—The functions and powers of the clergy—The lesser gods—Marduk—Ishtar—The Babylonian stories of the Creation and the Flood—The love of Ishtar and Tammuz—The descent of Ishtar into Hell—The death and resurrection of Tammuz—Ritual and prayer—Penitential psalms—Sin—Magic—Superstition

V. THE MORALS OF BABYLON, 244
Religion divorced from morals—Sacred prostitution—Free love—Marriage—Adultery—Divorce—The position of woman—The relaxation of morals

VI. LETTERS AND LITERATURE, 248
Cuneiform—Its decipherment—Language—Literature—The epic of Gilgamesh

XV

VII. ARTISTS, 254
The lesser arts—Music—Painting—Sculpture—Bas-relief—Architecture

VIII. BABYLONIAN SCIENCE, 256
Mathematics—Astronomy—The calendar—Geography—Medicine

IX. PHILOSOPHERS, 259
Religion and Philosophy—The Babylonian Job—The Babylonian Koheleth—An anti-clerical

X. EPITAPH, 263

Chapter X: ASSYRIA 265

I. CHRONICLES, 265
Beginnings — Cities — Race — The conquerors — Sennacherib and Esarhaddon — "Sardanapalus"

II. ASSYRIAN GOVERNMENT, 270
Imperialism—Assyrian war—The conscript gods—Law—Delicacies of penology—Administration—The violence of Oriental monarchies

III. ASSYRIAN LIFE, 274
Industry and trade—Marriage and morals—Religion and science—Letters and libraries—The Assyrian ideal of a gentleman

IV. ASSYRIAN ART, 278
Minor arts—Bas-relief—Statuary—Building—A page from "Sardanapalus"

V. ASSYRIA PASSES, 282
The last days of a king—Sources of Assyrian decay—The fall of Nineveh

Chapter XI: A MOTLEY OF NATIONS 285

I. THE INDO-EUROPEAN PEOPLES, 285
The ethnic scene—Mitannians—Hittites—Armenians—Scythians—Phrygians—The Divine Mother—Lydians—Crœsus—Coinage—Crœsus, Solon and Cyrus

II. THE SEMITIC PEOPLES, 290
The antiquity of the Arabs—Phœnicians—Their world trade—Their circumnavigation of Africa—Colonies—Tyre and Sidon—Deities—The dissemination of the alphabet—Syria—Astarte—The death and resurrection of Adoni—The sacrifice of children

Chapter XII: JUDEA 299

I. THE PROMISED LAND, 299
Palestine — Climate — Prehistory — Abraham's people — The Jews in Egypt — The Exodus — The conquest of Canaan

II. SOLOMON IN ALL HIS GLORY, 302
Race — Appearance — Language — Organization — Judges and kings — Saul — David —Solomon—His wealth—The Temple—Rise of the social problem in Israel

III. THE GOD OF HOSTS, 308
Polytheism—Yahveh—Henotheism—Character of the Hebrew religion—The idea of sin—Sacrifice—Circumcision—The priesthood—Strange gods

IV. THE FIRST RADICALS, 314

The class war—Origin of the Prophets—Amos at Jerusalem—Isaiah—His attacks upon the rich—His doctrine of a Messiah—The influence of the Prophets

V. THE DEATH AND RESURRECTION OF JERUSALEM, 320

The birth of the Bible—The destruction of Jerusalem—The Babylonian Captivity—Jeremiah—Ezekiel—The Second Isaiah—The liberation of the Jews—The Second Temple

VI. THE PEOPLE OF THE BOOK, 328

The "Book of the Law"—The composition of the Pentateuch—The myths of Genesis—The Mosaic Code—The Ten Commandments—The idea of God—The sabbath—The Jewish family—Estimate of the Mosaic legislation

VII. THE LITERATURE AND PHILOSOPHY OF THE BIBLE, 339

History — Fiction — Poetry — The Psalms — The Song of Songs — Proverbs — Job — The idea of immortality—The pessimism of Ecclesiastes—The advent of Alexander

Chapter XIII: PERSIA.. 350

I. THE RISE AND FALL OF THE MEDES, 350

Their origins—Rulers—The blood treaty of Sardis—Degeneration

II. THE GREAT KINGS, 352

The romantic Cyrus—His enlightened policies—Cambyses—Darius the Great—The invasion of Greece

III. PERSIAN LIFE AND INDUSTRY, 355

The empire—The people—The language—The peasants—The imperial highways—Trade and finance

IV. AN EXPERIMENT IN GOVERNMENT, 359

The king—The nobles—The army—Law—A savage punishment—The capitals—The satrapies—An achievement in administration

V. ZARATHUSTRA, 364

The coming of the Prophet—Persian religion before Zarathustra—The Bible of Persia—Ahura-Mazda—The good and the evil spirits—Their struggle for the possession of the world

VI. ZOROASTRIAN ETHICS, 368

Man as a battlefield—The Undying Fire—Hell, Purgatory and Paradise—The cult of Mithra—The Magi—The Parsees

VII. PERSIAN MANNERS AND MORALS, 373

Violence and honor—The code of cleanliness—Sins of the flesh—Virgins and bachelors—Marriage—Women—Children—Persian ideas of education

VIII. SCIENCE AND ART, 376

Medicine—Minor arts—The tombs of Cyrus and Darius—The palaces of Persepolis—The Frieze of the Archers—Estimate of Persian art

IX. DECADENCE, 381

How a nation may die—Xerxes—A paragraph of murders—Artaxerxes II—Cyrus the Younger—Darius the Little—Causes of decay: political, military, moral—Alexander conquers Persia, and advances upon India

BOOK TWO

INDIA AND HER NEIGHBORS

Chronological Table of Indian History... 389

Chapter XIV: THE FOUNDATIONS OF INDIA.................................... 391

    I. SCENE OF THE DRAMA, 391
      The rediscovery of India—A glance at the map—Climatic influences

    II. THE OLDEST CIVILIZATION?, 394
      Prehistoric India—Mohenjo-daro—Its antiquity

    III. THE INDO-ARYANS, 396
      The natives—The invaders—The village community—Caste—Warriors—Priests—Merchants—Workers—Outcastes

    IV. INDO-ARYAN SOCIETY, 399
      Herders—Tillers of the soil—Craftsmen—Traders—Coinage and credit—Morals—Marriage—Woman

    V. THE RELIGION OF THE *VEDAS*, 402
      Pre-Vedic religion—Vedic gods—Moral gods—The Vedic story of Creation—Immortality—The horse sacrifice

    VI. THE *VEDAS* AS LITERATURE, 405
      Sanskrit and English — Writing — The four *Vedas* — The *Rig-veda* — A Hymn of Creation

    VII. THE PHILOSOPHY OF THE *UPANISHADS*, 410
      The authors—Their theme—Intellect *vs.* intuition—Atman—Brahman—Their identity—A description of God—Salvation—Influence of the *Upanishads*—Emerson on Brahma

Chapter XV: BUDDHA.. 416

    I. THE HERETICS, 416
      Sceptics—Nihilists—Sophists—Atheists—Materialists—Religions without a god

    II. MAHAVIRA AND THE JAINS, 419
      The Great Hero—The Jain creed—Atheistic polytheism—Asceticism—Salvation by suicide—Later history of the Jains

    III. THE LEGEND OF BUDDHA, 422
      The background of Buddhism—The miraculous birth—Youth—The sorrows of life—Flight—Ascetic years—Enlightenment—A vision of *Nirvana*

    IV. THE TEACHING OF BUDDHA, 428
      Portrait of the Master—His methods—The Four Noble Truths—The Eightfold Way—The Five Moral Rules—Buddha and Christ—Buddha's agnosticism and anti-clericalism—His Atheism—His soul-less psychology—The meaning of *Nirvana*

    V. THE LAST DAYS OF BUDDHA, 436
      His miracles—He visits his father's house—The Buddhist monks—Death

Chapter XVI: FROM ALEXANDER TO AURANGZEB............................ 440

I. CHANDRAGUPTA, 440
Alexander in India — Chandragupta the liberator — The people — The university of
Taxila—The royal palace—A day in the life of a king—An older Machiavelli—Admin-
istration—Law—Public health—Transport and roads—Municipal government

II. THE PHILOSOPHER-KING, 446
Ashoka—The Edict of Tolerance—Ashoka's missionaries—His failure—His success

III. THE GOLDEN AGE OF INDIA, 450
An epoch of invasions—The Kushan kings—The Gupta Empire—The travels of Fa-
Hien—The revival of letters—The Huns in India—Harsha the generous—The travels
of Yuan Chwang

IV. ANNALS OF RAJPUTANA, 454
The Samurai of India—The age of chivalry—The fall of Chitor

V. THE ZENITH OF THE SOUTH, 456
The kingdoms of the Deccan—Vijayanagar—Krishna Raya—A medieval metropolis—
Laws—Arts—Religion—Tragedy

VI. THE MOSLEM CONQUEST, 459
The weakening of India—Mahmud of Ghazni—The Sultanate of Delhi—Its cultural
asides—Its brutal policy—The lesson of Indian history

VII. AKBAR THE GREAT, 463
Tamerlane—Babur—Humayun—Akbar—His government—His character—His patron-
age of the arts—His passion for philosophy—His friendship for Hinduism and Christianity—His new religion—The last days of Akbar

VIII. THE DECLINE OF THE MOGULS, 472
The children of great men — Jehangir — Shah Jehan — His magnificence — His fall —
Aurangzeb—His fanaticism—His death—The coming of the British

Chapter XVII: THE LIFE OF THE PEOPLE.. 477

I. THE MAKERS OF WEALTH, 477
The jungle background — Agriculture — Mining — Handicrafts — Commerce —
Money — Taxes — Famines — Poverty and wealth

II. THE ORGANIZATION OF SOCIETY, 482
The monarchy—Law—The Code of "Manu"—Development of the caste system—Rise
of the Brahmans—Their privileges and powers—Their obligations—In defense of caste

III. MORALS AND MARRIAGE, 488
Dharma — Children — Child marriage — The art of love — Prostitution — Romantic
love — Marriage — The family — Woman — Her intellectual life — Her rights —
Purdah — Suttee-The Widow

IV. MANNERS, CUSTOMS AND CHARACTER, 496
Sexual modesty—Hygiene—Dress—Appearance—The gentle art among the Hindus—
Faults and virtues—Games—Festivals—Death

CONTENTS

Chapter XVIII: THE PARADISE OF THE GODS...................................... 503

I. THE LATER HISTORY OF BUDDHISM, 503
The Zenith of Buddhism—The Two Vehicles—*Mahayana*—Buddhism, Stoicism and Christianity—The decay of Buddhism—Its migrations: Ceylon, Burma, Turkestan, Tibet, Cambodia, China, Japan

II. THE NEW DIVINITIES, 507
Hinduism—Brahma, Vishnu, Shiva—Krishna—Kali—Animal gods—The sacred cow—Polytheism and monotheism

III. BELIEFS, 511
The *Puranas*—The reincarnations of the universe—The migrations of the soul—*Karma*—Its philosophical aspects—Life as evil—Release

IV. CURIOSITIES OF RELIGION, 517
Superstitions — Astrology — Phallic worship — Ritual — Sacrifice — Purification — The sacred waters

V. SAINTS AND SCEPTICS, 522
Methods of sanctity—Heretics—Toleration—General view of Hindu religion

Chapter XIX: THE LIFE OF THE MIND... 526

I. HINDU SCIENCE, 526
Its religious origins — Astronomers — Mathematicians — The "Arabic" numerals — The decimal system — Algebra — Geometry — Physics — Chemistry — Physiology — Vedic medicine — Physicians — Surgeons — Anesthetics — Vaccination — Hypnotism

II. THE SIX SYSTEMS OF BRAHMANICAL PHILOSOPHY, 533
The antiquity of Indian philosophy—Its prominent rôle—Its scholars—Forms—Conception of orthodoxy—The assumptions of Hindu philosophy

1. THE *Nyaya* SYSTEM

2. THE *Vaisheshika* SYSTEM

3. THE *Sankhya* SYSTEM
Its high repute—Metaphysics—Evolution—Atheism—Idealism—Spirit—Body, mind and soul—The goal of philosophy—Influence of the *Sankhya*

4. THE *Yoga* SYSTEM
The Holy Men—The antiquity of *Yoga*—Its meaning—The eight stages of discipline—The aim of *Yoga*—The miracles of the *Yogi*—The sincerity of *Yoga*

5. THE *Purva Mimansa*

6. THE *Vedanta* SYSTEM
Origin — Shankara — Logic — Epistemology — *Maya* — Psychology — Theology — God — Ethics — Difficulties of the system — Death of Shankara

III. THE CONCLUSIONS OF HINDU PHILOSOPHY, 552
Decadence—Summary—Criticism—Influence

CONTENTS

Chapter XX: THE LITERATURE OF INDIA.................................... 555

I. THE LANGUAGES OF INDIA, 555
Sanskrit—The vernaculars—Grammar

II. EDUCATION, 556
Schools—Methods—Universities—Moslem education—An emperor on education

III. THE EPICS, 561
The *Mahabharata*—Its story—Its form—The *Bhagavad-Gita*—The metaphysics of war
—The price of freedom—The *Ramayana*—A forest idyl—The rape of Sita—The Hindu
epics and the Greek

IV. DRAMA, 571
Origins—*The Clay Cart*—Characteristics of Hindu drama—Kalidasa—The story of
Shakuntala—Estimate of Indian drama

V. PROSE AND POETRY, 577
Their unity in India—Fables—History—Tales—Minor poets—Rise of the vernacular
literature—Chandi Das—Tulsi Das—Poets of the south—Kabir

Chapter XXI: INDIAN ART.................................... 584

I. THE MINOR ARTS, 584
The great age of Indian art—Its uniqueness—Its association with industry—Pottery—
Metal—Wood—Ivory—Jewelry—Textiles

II. MUSIC, 586
A concert in India—Music and the dance—Musicians—Scale and forms—Themes—
Music and philosophy

III. PAINTING, 589
Prehistoric—The frescoes of Ajanta—Rajput miniatures—The Mogul school—The
painters—The theorists

IV. SCULPTURE, 593
Primitive—Buddhist—Gandhara—Gupta—"Colonial"—Estimate

V. ARCHITECTURE, 596
1. HINDU ARCHITECTURE
Before Ashoka—Ashokan—Buddhist—Jain—The masterpieces of the north—Their
destruction—The southern style—Monolithic temples—Structural temples

2. "COLONIAL" ARCHITECTURE
Ceylon — Java — Cambodia — The Khmers — Their religion — Angkor — Fall of
the Khmers — Siam — Burma

3. MOSLEM ARCHITECTURE IN INDIA
The Afghan style—The Mogul style—Delhi—Agra—The Taj Mahal

4. INDIAN ARCHITECTURE AND CIVILIZATION
Decay of Indian art—Hindu and Moslem architecture compared—General view of
Indian civilization

xxi

Chapter XXII: A CHRISTIAN EPILOGUE.............................. 613

   I. THE JOLLY BUCCANEERS, 613
     The arrival of the Europeans—The British Conquest—The Sepoy Mutiny—Advantages and disadvantages of British rule

   II. LATTER-DAY SAINTS, 615
     Christianity in India — The *Brahma-Somaj* — Mohammedanism — Ramakrishna — Vivekananda

   III. TAGORE, 618
     Science and art—A family of geniuses—Youth of Rabindranath—His poetry—His politics—His school

   IV. EAST IS WEST, 622
     Changing India—Economic changes—Social—The decaying caste system—Castes and guilds—Untouchables—The emergence of woman

   V. THE NATIONALIST MOVEMENT, 625
     The westernized students — The secularization of heaven — The Indian National Congress

   VI. MAHATMA GANDHI, 626
     Portrait of a saint—The ascetic—The Christian—The education of Gandhi—In Africa —The Revolt of 1921—"I am the man"—Prison years—*Young India*—The revolution of the spinning-wheel—The achievements of Gandhi

   VII. FAREWELL TO INDIA, 633
     The revivification of India—The gifts of India

BOOK THREE

THE FAR EAST

A. CHINA

Chronology of Chinese Civilization................................. 636

Chapter XXIII: THE AGE OF THE PHILOSOPHERS........................... 639

   I. THE BEGINNINGS, 639
     1. ESTIMATES OF THE CHINESE
     2. THE MIDDLE FLOWERY KINGDOM
       Geography—Race—Prehistory
     3. THE UNKNOWN CENTURIES
       The Creation according to China—The coming of culture—Wine and chopsticks —The virtuous emperors—A royal atheist
     4. THE FIRST CHINESE CIVILIZATION
       The Feudal Age in China—An able minister—The struggle between custom and law—Culture and anarchy—Love lyrics from the *Book of Odes*
     5. THE PRE-CONFUCIAN PHILOSOPHERS
       The *Book of Changes*—The *yang* and the *yin*—The Chinese Enlightenment—Teng Shih, the Socrates of China

6. THE OLD MASTER

Lao-tze—The *Tao*—On intellectuals in government—The foolishness of laws—A Rousseauian Utopia and a Christian ethic—Portrait of a wise man—The meeting of Lao-tze and Confucius

II. CONFUCIUS, 658

1. THE SAGE IN SEARCH OF A STATE

Birth and youth—Marriage and divorce—Pupils and methods—Appearance and character—The lady and the tiger—A definition of good government—Confucius in office—Wander-years—The consolations of old age

2. THE NINE CLASSICS

3. THE AGNOSTICISM OF CONFUCIUS

A fragment of logic—The philosopher and the urchins—A formula of wisdom

4. THE WAY OF THE HIGHER MAN

Another portrait of the sage—Elements of character—The Golden Rule

5. CONFUCIAN POLITICS

Popular sovereignty—Government by example—The decentralization of wealth—Music and manners—Socialism and revolution

6. THE INFLUENCE OF CONFUCIUS

The Confucian scholars—Their victory over the Legalists—Defects of Confucianism—The contemporaneity of Confucius

III. SOCIALISTS AND ANARCHISTS, 677

1. MO TI, ALTRUIST

2. YANG CHU, EGOIST

3. MENCIUS, MENTOR OF PRINCES

A model mother—A philosopher among kings—Are men by nature good?—Single tax—Mencius and the communists—The profit-motive—The right of revolution

4. HSUN-TZE, REALIST

The evil nature of man—The necessity of law

5. CHUANG-TZE, IDEALIST

The Return to Nature—Governmentless society—The Way of Nature—The limits of the intellect—The evolution of man—The Button-Moulder—The influence of Chinese philosophy in Europe

Chapter XXIV: THE AGE OF THE POETS... 694

I. CHINA'S BISMARCK, 694

The Period of Contending States—The suicide of Ch'u P'ing—Shih Huang-ti unifies China—The Great Wall—The "Burning of the Books"—The failure of Shih Huang-ti

II. EXPERIMENTS IN SOCIALISM, 698

Chaos and poverty—The Han Dynasty—The reforms of Wu Ti—The income tax—The planned economy of Wang Mang—Its overthrow—The Tatar invasion

III. THE GLORY OF T'ANG, 701

The new dynasty—T'ai Tsung's method of reducing crime—An age of prosperity—The "Brilliant Emperor"—The romance of Yang Kwei-fei—The rebellion of An Lu-shan

IV. THE BANISHED ANGEL, 705

An anecdote of Li Po—His youth, prowess and loves—On the imperial barge—The gospel of the grape—War—The wanderings of Li Po—In prison—"Deathless Poetry"

V. SOME QUALITIES OF CHINESE POETRY, 711

"Free verse"—"Imagism"—"Every poem a picture and every picture a poem"—Sentimentality—Perfection of form

VI. TU FU, 713

T'ao Ch'ien—Po Chü-i—Poems for malaria—Tu Fu and Li Po—A vision of war—Prosperous days—Destitution—Death

VII. PROSE, 717

The abundance of Chinese literature—Romances—History—Szuma Ch'ien—Essays—Han Yü on the bone of Buddha

VIII. THE STAGE, 721

Its low repute in China—Origins—The play—The audience—The actors—Music

Chapter XXV: THE AGE OF THE ARTISTS... 724

I. THE SUNG RENAISSANCE, 724

1. THE SOCIALISM OF WANG AN-SHIH

The Sung Dynasty—A radical premier—His cure for unemployment—The regulation of industry—Codes of wages and prices—The nationalization of commerce—State insurance against unemployment, poverty and old age—Examinations for public office—The defeat of Wang An-shih

2. THE REVIVAL OF LEARNING

The growth of scholarship—Paper and ink in China—Steps in the invention of printing—The oldest book—Paper money—Movable type—Anthologies, dictionaries, encyclopedias.

3. THE REBIRTH OF PHILOSOPHY

Chu Hsi—Wang Yang-ming—Beyond good and evil

II. BRONZES, LACQUER AND JADE, 735

The rôle of art in China—Textiles—Furniture—Jewelry—Fans—The making of lacquer—The cutting of jade—Some masterpieces in bronze—Chinese sculpture

III. PAGODAS AND PALACES, 740

Chinese architecture—The Porcelain Tower of Nanking—The Jade Pagoda of Peking — The Temple of Confucius — The Temple and Altar of Heaven — The palaces of Kublai Khan—A Chinese home—The interior—Color and form

IV. PAINTING, 745

1. MASTERS OF CHINESE PAINTING

Ku K'ai-chhi, the "greatest painter, wit and fool"—Han Yü's miniature—The classic and the romantic schools—Wang Wei—Wu Tao-tze—Hui Tsung, the artist-emperor—Masters of the Sung age

2. QUALITIES OF CHINESE PAINTING

The rejection of perspective—Of realism—Line as nobler than color—Form as rhythm—Representation by suggestion—Conventions and restrictions—Sincerity of Chinese art

V. PORCELAIN, 754

The ceramic art—The making of porcelain—Its early history—*Céladon*—Enamels—The skill of Hao Shih-chiu—*Cloisonné*—The age of K'ang-hsi—Of Ch'ien Lung

Chapter XXVI: THE PEOPLE AND THE STATE.................................... 760

I. HISTORICAL INTERLUDE, 760

  1. MARCO POLO VISITS KUBLAI KHAN
  The incredible travelers—Adventures of a Venetian in China—The elegance and prosperity of Hangchow—The palaces of Peking—The Mongol Conquest—Jenghiz Khan—Kublai Khan—His character and policy—His harem—"Marco Millions"

  2. THE MING AND THE CH'ING
  Fall of the Mongols — The Ming Dynasty — The Manchu invasion — The Ch'ing Dynasty—An enlightened monarch—Ch'ien Lung rejects the Occident

II. THE PEOPLE AND THEIR LANGUAGE, 769

Population—Appearance—Dress—Peculiarities of Chinese speech—Of Chinese writing

III. THE PRACTICAL LIFE, 774

  1. IN THE FIELDS
  The poverty of the peasant — Methods of husbandry — Crops — Tea — Food — The stoicism of the village

  2. IN THE SHOPS
  Handicrafts — Silk — Factories — Guilds — Men of burden — Roads and canals – Merchants—Credit and coinage—Currency experiments—Printing-press inflation

  3. INVENTION AND SCIENCE
  Gunpowder, fireworks and war—The compass—Poverty of industrial invention-- Geography—Mathematics—Physics—*Feng shui*—Astronomy—Medicine—Hygiene

IV. RELIGION WITHOUT A CHURCH, 783

Superstition and scepticism—Animism—The worship of Heaven—Ancestor-worship— Confucianism—Taoism—The elixir of immortality—Buddhism—Religious toleration and eclecticism—Mohammedanism—Christianity—Causes of its failure in China

V. THE RULE OF MORALS, 788

The high place of morals in Chinese society—The family—Children—Chastity—Prostitution—Premarital relations—Marriage and love—Monogamy and polygamy—Concubinage — Divorce — A Chinese empress — The patriarchal male — The subjection of woman—The Chinese character

VI. A GOVERNMENT PRAISED BY VOLTAIRE, 795

The submergence of the individual—Self-government—The village and the province— The laxity of the law—The severity of punishment—The Emperor—The Censor—Administrative boards—Education for public office—Nomination by education—The examination system—Its defects—Its virtues

Chapter XXVII: REVOLUTION AND RENEWAL.................................... 803

    I. THE WHITE PERIL, 803
    The conflict of Asia and Europe—The Portuguese—The Spanish—The Dutch—The
    English—The opium trade—The Opium Wars—The T'ai-p'ing Rebellion—The War
    with Japan—The attempt to dismember China—The "Open Door"—The Empress
    Dowager—The reforms of Kuang Hsu—His removal from power—The "Boxers"—
    The Indemnity

    II. THE DEATH OF A CIVILIZATION, 808
    The Indemnity students—Their Westernization—Their disintegrative effect in China
    —The rôle of the missionary—Sun Yat-sen, the Christian—His youthful adventures—
    His meeting with Li Hung-chang—His plans for a revolution—Their success—Yuan
    Shi-k'ai—The death of Sun Yat-sen—Chaos and village—Communism—"The north
    pacified"—Chiang Kai-shek—Japan in Manchuria—At Shanghai

    III. BEGINNINGS OF A NEW ORDER, 814
    Change in the village—In the town—The factories—Commerce—Labor unions—Wages
    —The new government—Nationalism vs. Westernization—The dethronement of Con-
    fucius—The reaction against religion—The new morality—Marriage in transition—
    Birth control—Co-education—The "New Tide" in literature and philosophy—The
    new language of literature—Hu Shih—Elements of destruction—Elements of renewal

B. JAPAN

Chronology of Japanese Civilization................................ 826

Chapter XXVIII: THE MAKERS OF JAPAN..................................... 829

    I. THE CHILDREN OF THE GODS, 829
    How Japan was created—The rôle of earthquakes

    II. PRIMITIVE JAPAN, 831
    Racial components—Early civilization—Religion—Shinto—Buddhism—The beginnings
    of art—The "Great Reform"

    III. THE IMPERIAL AGE, 834
    The emperors—The aristocracy—The influence of China—The Golden Age of
    Kyoto—Decadence

    IV. THE DICTATORS, 836
    The shoguns—The Kamakura Bakufu—The Hojo Regency—Kublai Khan's inva-
    sion—The Ashikaga Shogunate—The three buccaneers

    V. GREAT MONKEY-FACE, 838
    The rise of Hideyoshi—The attack upon Korea—The conflict with Christianity

    VI. THE GREAT SHOGUN, 841
    The accession of Iyeyasu—His philosophy—Iyeyasu and Christianity—Death of
    Iyeyasu—The Tokugawa Shogunate

Chapter XXIX: THE POLITICAL AND MORAL FOUNDATIONS............. 845

I. THE SAMURAI, 845

The powerless emperor—The powers of the *shogun*—The sword of the *Samurai*—The code of the *Samurai*—*Hara-kiri*—The Forty-seven *Ronin*—A commuted sentence

II. THE LAW, 850

The first code—Group responsibility—Punishments

III. THE TOILERS, 851

Castes—An experiment in the nationalization of land—State fixing of wages—A famine—Handicrafts—Artisans and guilds

IV. THE PEOPLE, 854

Stature—Cosmetics—Costume—Diet—Etiquette—*Saki*—The tea ceremony—The flower ceremony—Love of nature—Gardens—Homes

V. THE FAMILY, 860

The paternal autocrat—The status of woman—Children—Sexual morality—The *Geisha*—Love

VI. THE SAINTS, 863

Religion in Japan—The transformation of Buddhism—The priests—Sceptics

VII. THE THINKERS, 866

Confucius reaches Japan—A critic of religion—The religion of scholarship—Kaibara Ekken—On education—On pleasure—The rival schools—A Japanese Spinoza—Ito Jinsai—Ito Togai—Ogyu Sorai—The war of the scholars—Mabuchi—Moto-ori

Chapter XXX: THE MIND AND ART OF OLD JAPAN........................ 876

I. LANGUAGE AND EDUCATION, 876

The language—Writing—Education

II. POETRY, 878

The *Manyoshu*—The *Kokinshu*—Characteristics of Japanese poetry—Examples—The game of poetry—The *hokka*-gamblers

III. PROSE, 881

1. FICTION

Lady Muraski—The *Tale of Genji*—Its excellence—Later Japanese fiction—A humorist

2. HISTORY

The historians—Arai Hakuseki

3. THE ESSAY

The Lady Sei Shonagon—Kamo no-Chomei

IV. THE DRAMA, 889

The *No* plays—Their character—The popular stage—The Japanese Shakespeare—Summary judgment

V. THE ART OF LITTLE THINGS, 891

Creative imitation—Music and the dance—*Inro* and *netsuke*—Hidari Jingaro—Lacquer

VI. ARCHITECTURE, 894
Temples—Palaces—The shrine of Iyeyasu—Homes

VII. METALS AND STATUES, 896
Swords—Mirrors—The Trinity of Horiuji—Colossi—Religion and sculpture

VIII. POTTERY, 899
The Chinese stimulus—The potters of Hizen—Pottery and tea—How Goto Saijiro brought the art of porcelain from Hizen to Kaga—The nineteenth century

IX. PAINTING, 901
Difficulties of the subject—Methods and materials—Forms and ideals—Korean origins and Buddhist inspiration—The Tosa School—The return to China—Sesshiu—The Kano School—Koyetsu and Korin—The Realistic School

X. PRINTS, 907
The *Ukiyoye* School—Its founders—Its masters—Hokusai—Hiroshige

XI. JAPANESE ART AND CIVILIZATION, 910
A retrospect—Contrasts—An estimate—The doom of the old Japan

Chapter XXXI: THE NEW JAPAN.. 914

I. THE POLITICAL REVOLUTION, 914
The decay of the Shogunate—America knocks at the door—The Restoration—The Westernization of Japan—Political reconstruction—The new constitution—Law—The army—The war with Russia—Its political results

II. THE INDUSTRIAL REVOLUTION, 919
Industrialization—Factories—Wages—Strikes—Poverty—The Japanese point of view

III. THE CULTURAL REVOLUTION, 922
Changes in dress—In manners—The Japanese character—Morals and marriage in transition—Religion—Science—Japanese medicine—Art and taste—Language and education—Naturalistic fiction—New forms of poetry

IV. THE NEW EMPIRE, 927
The precarious bases of the new civilization—Causes of Japanese imperialism—The Twenty-one Demands—The Washington Conference—The Immigration Act of 1924—The invasion of Manchuria—The new kingdom—Japan and Russia—Japan and Europe—Must America fight Japan?

Envoi: Our Oriental Heritage.. 934

Glossary of Foreign Terms.. 939

Bibliography of Books Referred to in the Text............................ 945

Notes 956

Pronouncing and Biographical Index...................................... 1001

List of Illustrations

(Illustration Section follows page xxxii)

Cover Design: The god Shamash transmits a code of laws to Hammurabi
From a cylinder in The Louvre

FIG. 1. Granite statue of Rameses II
Turin Museum, Italy

FIG. 2. Bison painted in paleolithic cave at Altamira, Spain
Photo by American Museum of Natural History

FIG. 3. Hypothetical reconstruction of a neolithic lake dwelling
American Museum of Natural History

FIG. 4. Development of the alphabet

FIG. 5. Stele of Naram-sin
Louvre; photo by Archives Photographiques d'Art et d'Histoire

FIG. 6. The "little" Gudea
Louvre; photo by Metropolitan Museum of Art

FIG. 7. Temple of Der-el-Bahri
Photo by Lindsley F. Hall

FIG. 8. Colonnade and court of the temple at Luxor
Photo by Metropolitan Museum of Art

FIG. 9. Hypothetical reconstruction of the Hypostyle Hall at Karnak
From a model in the Metropolitan Museum of Art

FIG. 10. Colonnade of the Hypostyle Hall at Karnak
Underwood & Underwood

FIG. 11. The Rosetta Stone
British Museum

FIG. 12. Diorite head of the Pharaoh Khafre
Cairo Museum; photo by Metropolitan Museum of Art

FIG. 13. The seated Scribe
Louvre; photo by Metropolitan Museum of Art

FIG. 14. Wooden figure of the "Sheik-el-Beled"
Cairo Museum; photo by Metropolitan Museum of Art

FIG. 15. Sandstone head from the workshop of the sculptor Thutmose at Amarna
State Museum, Berlin; photo by Metropolitan Museum of Art

FIG. 16. Head of a king, probably Senusret III.
Metropolitan Museum of Art

FIG. 17. The royal falcon and serpent. Limestone relief from First Dynasty
Louvre; photo by Metropolitan Museum of Art

FIG. 18. Head of Thutmose III
Cairo Museum; photo by Metropolitan Museum of Art

FIG. 19. Rameses II presenting an offering
Cairo Museum; photo by Metropolitan Museum of Art

FIG. 20. Bronze figure of the Lady Tekoschet
Athens Museum; photo by Metropolitan Museum of Art

FIG. 21. Seated figure of Montumihait
State Museum, Berlin

FIG. 22. Colossi of Rameses II, with life-size figures of Queen Nofretete at his feet, at the cave temple of Abu Simbel
Ewing Galloway, N. Y.

FIG. 23. The dancing girl. Design on an ostracon
Turin Museum, Italy

FIG. 24. Cat watching his prey. A wall-painting in the grave of Khnumho-tep at Beni-Hasan
Copy by Howard Carter; courtesy of Egypt Exploration Society

FIG. 25. Chair of Tutenkhamon
Cairo Museum; photo by Metropolitan Museum of Art

FIG. 26. Painted limestone head of Ikhnaton's Queen Nofretete
Metropolitan Museum of Art facsimile of original in State Museum, Berlin

FIG. 27. The god Shamash transmits a code of laws to Hammurabi
Louvre; photo copyright by W. A. Mansell & Co., London

FIG. 28. The "Lion of Babylon." Painted tile-relief
State Museum, Berlin; Courtesy of the Metropolitan Museum of Art

FIG. 29. Head of Esarhaddon
State Museum, Berlin

FIG. 30. The Prism of Sennacherib
Iraq Museum; courtesy of the Oriental Institute, University of Chicago

FIG. 31. The Dying Lioness of Nineveh
British Museum; photo by Metropolitan Museum of Art

FIG. 32. The Lion Hunt; relief on alabaster, from Nineveh
British Museum; photo by Metropolitan Museum of Art

FIG. 33. Assyrian relief of Marduk fighting Tiamat, from Kalakh
British Museum; photo copyright by W. A. Mansell, London

FIG. 34. Winged Bull from the palace of Ashurnasirpal II at Kalakh
Metropolitan Museum of Art

FIG. 35. A street in Jerusalem

FIG. 36. Hypothetical restoration of Solomon's Temple
Underwood & Underwood

FIG. 37. The ruins of Persepolis
Courtesy of the Oriental Institute, University of Chicago

FIG. 38. "Frieze of the Archers." Painted tile-relief from Susa
Louvre; photo by Archives Photographiques d'Art et d'Histoire

FIG. 39. Burning Ghat at Calcutta
Bronson de Cou, from Ewing Galloway, N. Y.

FIG. 40. "Holy Men" at Benares

FIG. 41. A fresco at Ajanta

FIG. 42. Mogul painting of Durbar of Akbar at Akbarabad. Ca. 1620
Boston Museum of Fine Arts

FIG. 43. Torso of a youth, from Sanchi
Victoria and Albert Museum, London

FIG. 44. Seated statue of Brahma, 10th century
Metropolitan Museum of Art

FIG. 45. The Buddha of Sarnath, 5th century
        Photo by A. K. Coomaraswamy
FIG. 46. The Naga-King. Façade relief on Ajanta Cave-temple XIX
        Courtesy of A. K. Coomaraswamy
FIG. 47. The Dancing Shiva. South India, 17th century
        Minneapolis Institute of Arts
FIG. 48. The Three-faced Shiva, or Trimurti, Elephanta
        Underwood & Underwood
FIG. 49. The Buddha of Anuradhapura, Ceylon
        Ewing Galloway, N. Y.
FIG. 50. Lion capital of Ashoka column
        Sarnath Museum, Benares; copyright Archaeological Survey of India
FIG. 51. Sanchi Tope, north gate
        Underwood & Underwood
FIG. 52. Façade of the Gautami-Putra Monastery at Nasik
        India Office, London
FIG. 53. *Chaitya* hall interior, Cave XXVI, Ajanta.
FIG. 54. Interior of dome of the Tejahpala Temple at Mt. Abu
        Johnston & Hoffman, Calcutta
FIG. 55. Temple of Vimala Sah at Mt. Abu
        Underwood & Underwood
FIG. 56. Cave XIX, Ajanta
        Indian State Railways
FIG. 57. Elephanta Caves, near Bombay
        By Cowling, from Ewing Galloway, N. Y.
FIG. 58. The rock-cut Temple of Kailasha
        Indian State Railways
FIG. 59. Guardian deities, Temple of Elura
        Indian State Railways
FIG. 60. Façade, Angkor Wat, Indo-China
        Publishers' Photo Service
FIG. 61. Northeast end of Angkor Wat, Indo-China
        Publishers' Photo Service
FIG. 62. Rabindranath Tagore
        Underwood & Underwood
FIG. 63. Ananda Palace at Pagan, Burma
        Underwood & Underwood
FIG. 64. The Taj Mahal, Agra
        Ewing Galloway, N. Y.
FIG. 65. Imperial jewel casket of blue lacquer
        Underwood & Underwood
FIG. 66. The lacquered screen of K'ang-hsi
        Victoria and Albert Museum, London
FIG. 67. A bronze Kuan-yin of the Sui period
        Metropolitan Museum of Art
FIG. 68. Summer Palace, Peiping
FIG. 69. Temple of Heaven, Peiping
        Publishers' Photo Service

FIG. 70. Portraits of Thirteen Emperors. Attributed to Yen Li-pen, 7th century
Boston Museum of Fine Arts

FIG. 71. The Silk-beaters. By the Emperor Hui Tsung (1101-26)
Boston Museum of Fine Arts

FIG. 72. Landscape with Bridge and Willows. Ma Yuan, 12th century
Boston Museum of Fine Arts

FIG. 73. A hawthorn vase from the K'ang-hsi period
Metropolitan Museum of Art

FIG. 74. *Geisha* girls
Ewing Galloway, N. Y.

FIG. 75. Kiyomizu Temple, Kyoto, once a favorite resort of Japanese suicides
Underwood & Underwood

FIG. 76. Yo-mei-mon Gate, Nikko

FIG. 77. The Monkeys of Nikko. "Hear no evil, speak no evil, see no evil"
Ewing Galloway, N. Y.

FIG. 78. Image of Amida-Buddha at Horiuji
Photo by Metropolitan Museum of Art

FIG. 79. The bronze halo and background of the Amida at Horiuji.
Photo by Metropolitan Museum of Art

FIG. 80. The Vairochana Buddha of Japan. Carved and lacquered wood. Ca. 950 A.D.
Metropolitan Museum of Art

FIG. 81. The Daibutsu, or Great Buddha, at Kamakura

FIG. 82. Monkeys and Birds. By Sesshiu, 15th century

FIG. 83. A wave screen by Korin
Metropolitan Museum of Art

FIG. 84. The Falls of Yoro. By Hokusai
Metropolitan Museum of Art

FIG. 85. Foxes. By Hiroshige
Metropolitan Museum of Art

Maps of Egypt, the ancient Near East, India, and the Far East
will be found on the inside covers

Illustration Section

FIG. 1—*Granite statue of Rameses II*
Turin Museum, Italy

(See pages 188, 213)

FIG. 2—*Bison painted in paleolithic cave at Altamira, Spain*
Photo by American Museum of Natural History

(See page 96)

FIG. 3—*Hypothetical reconstruction of a neolithic lake dwelling*
American Museum of Natural History

(See page 98)

ENGLISH	EGYPTIAN HIEROGLYPH	ABU-SIMBEL	MOABITE STONE	IONIAN GREEK
A	ᛩ	◁	⪡	△ A
B	⬚ ▭	B B	⟆	B
G	𐄘		⟋	Γ Γ
D			◁	△
E		Ϝ E	⪫	Ϝ E
F(W)			Y	
Z	Y		Z	
H		日	日	日
TH			⊗	⊗
I		Ɩ	ﬧ	ǀ
K			⅄	K
L		ᴦ∧	ᒪ	⌐
M		∧	ᙏ	M
N	⬳	N	⅁	ᴎᴎN
X(SH)	⬳		≢	Ɫ
O		°◊O	○	○⌐
P	⌇⌇	⌐	7	⌐
S	⬳		ᒣ	
Q	⬳	Q	φ	
R	⬳		◁	P D
S	⬳	⟨⟨	w	⟨⟨⟩⟩
T	⬳	T	X	T
Ü				Y
P-H				
KH	⬳			X
PS				Ψ Ψ
ô				⌒

FIG. 4—*Development of the alphabet*

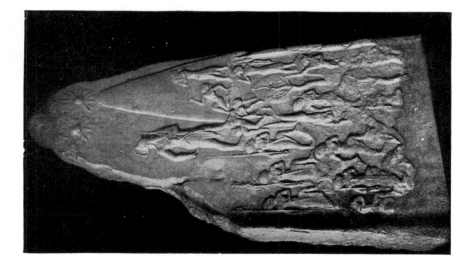

Fig. 5—Stele of
Naram-sin
Louvre; photo
by Archives
Photographiques
d'Art et
d'Histoire

(See page 122)

Fig. 6—The
"little" Gudea
Louvre; photo
by Metropolitan
Museum of Art

(See page 122)

FIG. 7—*Temple of Der-el-Bahri*
Photo by Lindsley F. Hall

(See page 154)

FIG. 8—*Colonnade and court of the temple at Luxor*
Photo by Metropolitan Museum of Art

(See page 142)

FIG. 9—*Hypothetical reconstruction of the Hypostyle Hall at Karnak*
From a model in the Metropolitan Museum of Art

FIG. 10—*Colonnade of the Hypostyle Hall at Karnak*
Underwood & Underwood

(See page 143)

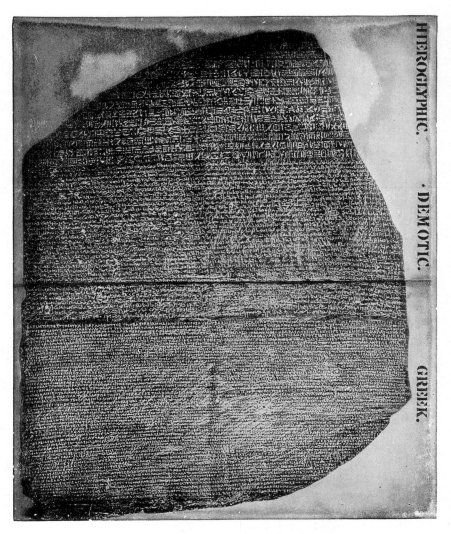

HIEROGLYPHIC.

DEMOTIC.

GREEK.

FIG. 11—*The Rosetta Stone*
British Museum

(See page 145)

FIG. 12—*Diorite head of the Pharaoh Khafre*
Cairo Museum; photo by Metropolitan Museum of Art

(See pages 148, 186)

FIG. 13—*The seated Scribe*

Louvre; photo by Metropolitan Museum **of Art**

(See pages 161, 186)

Fig. 14—
*Wooden figure
of the
"Sheik-el-Beled"*
Cairo Museum;
photo by Metro-
politan Museum
of Art

(See pages 168, 186)

FIG. 15—*Sandstone head from the workshop of the sculptor Thutmose at Amarna*
State Museum, Berlin; photo by Metropolitan Museum of Art

FIG. 16—*Head of a king, probably Senusret III*
Metropolitan Museum of Art

FIG. 17—*The royal falcon and serpent. Limestone relief from First Dynasty*
Louvre; photo by Metropolitan Museum of Art

FIG. 18—*Head of Thutmose III*
Cairo Museum; photo by Metropolitan Museum of Art

(See pages 184-190)

FIG. 19—*Rameses II presenting an offering*
Cairo Museum; photo by Metropolitan Museum of Art

FIG. 20—*Bronze figure of the
Lady Tekoschet*
Athens Museum; photo by Metro-
politan Museum of Art

FIG. 21—*Seated figure of
Montumihait*
State Museum, Berlin

(See pages 188-9)

FIG. 22—Colossi of Rameses II, with life-size figures of Queen Nefretere at his feet, at the cave temple of Abu Simbel

Ewing Galloway, N. Y.

(See page 188)

Fig. 23—*The dancing girl. Design on an ostracon*
Turin Museum, Italy

(See page 191)

Fig. 24—*Cat watching his prey. A wall-painting in the grave of Khnumhotep
at Beni-Hasan*
Copy by Howard Carter; courtesy of Egypt Exploration Society

(See page 190)

FIG. 25—*Chair of Tutenkhamon*
Cairo Museum; photo by Metropolitan Museum of Art

(See page 191)

FIG. 26—*Painted limestone head of Ikhnaton's Queen Nofretete*
Metropolitan Museum of Art facsimile of original in State Museum, Berlin

(See page 188)

FIG. 27—*The god Shamash transmits a code of laws to Hammurabi*
Louvre; photo copyright W. A. Mansell & Co., London

(See page 219)

FIG. 28—*The "Lion of Babylon." Painted tile-relief*
State Museum, Berlin; courtesy of the Metropolitan Museum of Art

(*See pages 254-5*)

FIG. 29—*Head of Esarhaddon*
State Museum, Berlin

(*See page* 281)

FIG. 30—*The Prism of Sennacherib*
Iraq Museum; courtesy of the Oriental Institute, University of Chicago

(See Chapter X)

FIG. 31–*The Dying Lioness of Nineveh*
British Museum; photo by Metropolitan Museum of Art

(*See page 279*)

FIG. 32—*The Lion Hunt; relief on alabaster, from Nineveh*
British Museum; Metropolitan Museum of Art

(See page 279)

FIG. 33—*Assyrian relief of Marduk fighting Tiamat, from Kalakh*
British Museum; photo copyright by W. A. Mansell, London

(See page 278)

FIG. 34–*Winged Bull from the palace of Ashurnasirpal II at Kalakh*
Metropolitan Museum of Art

(See page 279)

FIG. 35—*A street in Jerusalem*

FIG. 36—*Hypothetical restoration of Solomon's Temple*
Underwood & Underwood

(See page 307)

FIG. 37—*The ruins of Persepolis*
Courtesy of the Oriental Institute, University of Chicago

(*See page 379*)

Fig. 38—*"Frieze of the Archers." Painted tile-relief from Susa*
Louvre; photo by Archives Photographiques d'Art et d'Histoire

(See page 380)

FIG. 39—*Burning Ghat at Calcutta*
Bronson de Cou, from Ewing Galloway, N. Y.

(See page 521)

FIG. 40—*"Holy Men" at Benares*

(See page 52?)

FIG. 41—*A fresco at Ajanta*

(*See pages 589-90*)

FIG. 42—*Mogul painting of Durbar of Akbar at Akbarabad. Ca. 1620*
Boston Museum of Fine Arts

(See page 591)

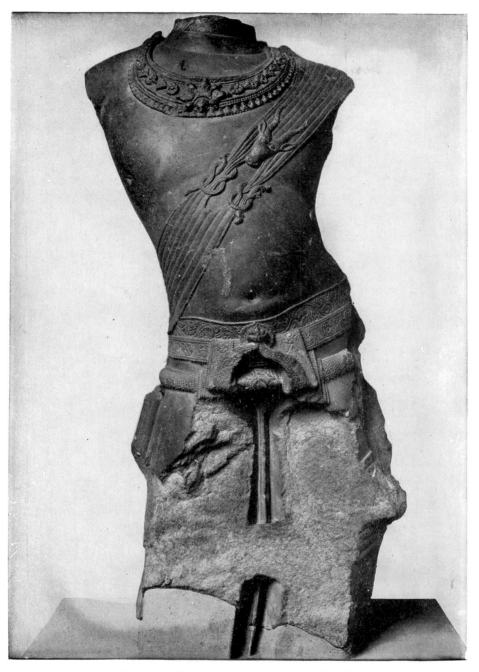

Fig. 43—*Torso of a youth, from Sanchi*
Victoria and Albert Museum, London

(See pages 593-6)

FIG. 44—*Seated statue of
Brahma, 10th century*
Metropolitan Museum of Art

FIG. 46—*The Naga-King.
Façade relief on Ajanta
Cave-temple XIX*
Courtesy of
A. K. Coomaraswamy

FIG. 45—*The Buddha of
Sarnath, 5th century*
Photo by A. K. Coomaraswamy

(See pages 593-6)

FIG. 47—*The Dancing Shiva. South India, 17th century*
Minneapolis Institute of Arts

(See page 594)

FIG. 48—*The Three-faced Shiva, or Trimurti, Elephanta*

Underwood & Underwood

(See page 594)

FIG. 49.—*The Buddha of Anuradhapura, Ceylon*
Ewing Galloway, N. Y.

(See page 595)

FIG. 50—*Lion capital of Ashoka column*
Sarnath Museum, Benares; copyright Archaeological Survey of India

(See page 596)

FIG. 51—*Sanchi Tope, north gate*
Underwood & Underwood

(See page 597)

FIG. 52—*Façade of the Gautami-Putra Monastery at Nasik*
India Office, London

(See page 597)

FIG. 53—*Chaitya hall interior, Cave XXVI, Ajanta*

(See page 598)

FIG. 54—*Interior of dome of the Tejahpala Temple at Mt. Abu*
Johnston & Hoffman, Calcutta

(*See page 598*)

FIG. 55—*Temple of Vimala Sah at Mt. Abu*
Underwood & Underwood

(See page 598)

Fig. 56—*Cave XIX, Ajanta*
Indian State Railways

(See page 598)

FIG. 57—*Elephanta Caves, near Bombay*
By Cowling, from Ewing Galloway, N. Y.

(See page 596)

FIG. 58—*The rock-cut Temple of Kailasha*
Indian State Railways

(See page 601)

FIG. 59—*Guardian deities, Temple of Elura*
Indian State Railways

(See page 601.)

Fig. 60—*Façade, Angkor Wat, Indo-China*
Publishers' Photo Service

(*See pages 604-5*)

FIG. 61—*Northeast end of Angkor Wat, Indo-China*
Publishers' Photo Service

(*See pages 604-5*)

FIG. 62—*Rabindranath Tagore*
Underwood & Underwood

(See page 619)

FIG. 63—*Ananda Palace at Pagan, Burma*
Underwood & Underwood

(See page 606)

FIG. 64—*The Taj Mahal, Agra*
Ewing Galloway, N. Y.

(See page 609)

FIG. 65—*Imperial jewel casket of blue lacquer*
Underwood & Underwood

(See page 736)

FIG. 66—*The lacquered screen of K'ang-hsi*
Victoria and Albert Museum, London

(See page 736)

FIG. 67—*A bronze Kuan-yin of the Sui period*
Metropolitan Museum of Art

(See page 738)

FIG. 68—*Summer
Palace, Peiping*

(See page 742)

FIG. 69—*Templc
of Heaven,
Peiping*
Publishers' Photo
Service

(See page 742)

FIG. 70—
Portraits of
Thirteen
Emperors.
Attributed to
Yen Li-pen,
7th century
Boston Museum
of Fine Arts

(See pages 745-52)

FIG. 71—*The Silk-beaters. By the Emperor Hui Tsung* (*1101-26*) Boston Museum of Fine Arts

(*See page 750*)

FIG. 72—*Landscape with Bridge and Willows. Ma Yuan, 12th century* Boston Museum of Fine Arts

(*See page 751*)

FIG. 73—*A hawthorn vase from the K'ang-hsi period*
Metropolitan Museum of Art

(See page 758)

FIG. 74—*Geisha girls*
Ewing Galloway, N. Y.

(*See page 862*)

FIG. 75—*Kiyomizu Temple, Kyoto, once a favorite resort of Japanese suicides*
Underwood & Underwood

(See page 895)

FIG. 76—*Yo-mei-mon Gate, Nikko*

(See page 895)

FIG. 77—*The Monkeys of Nikko.* "*Hear no evil, speak no evil, see no evil*"
Ewing Galloway, N. Y.

(*See page 895*)

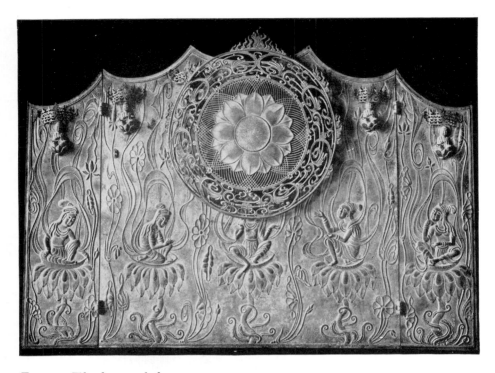

FIG. 79—*The bronze halo
and background of the
Amida at Horiuji*
Photo by
Metropolitan Museum of Art

(See page 897)

FIG. 78—*Image of Amida-
Buddha at Horiuji*
Photo by
Metropolitan Museum of Art

(See page 897)

FIG. 80—*The Vairochana Buddha of Japan. Carved and lacquered wood.*
Ca. 950 A.D.
Metropolitan Museum of Art

(See pages 896-8)

FIG. 81—*The Daibutsu, or Great Buddha, at Kamakura*

(See page 898)

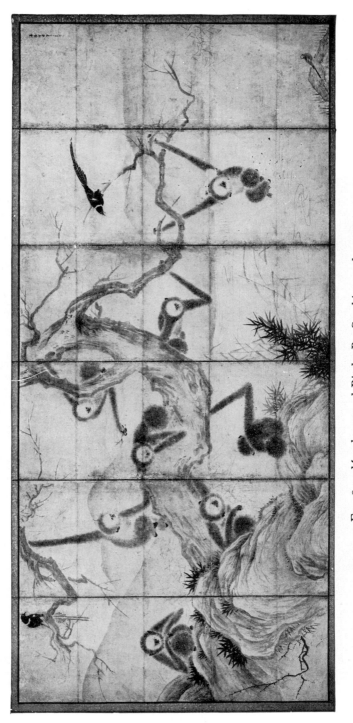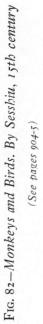

FIG. 82—*Monkeys and Birds. By Sesshiu, 15th century*

(*See pages 904-5*)

FIG. 83—*A wave screen*
by Korin
Metropolitan Museum
of Art

(*See page 906*)

FIG. 85—*Foxes. By Hiroshige*
Metropolitan Museum of Art

FIG. 84—*The Falls of Yoro. By Hokusai*
Metropolitan Museum of Art

(*See pages 907-10*)